THE TECH-HEAD GUIDE

MAVIC PRO

D1385511

DRONES

WILLIAM POTTER

First published in Great Britain in 2020
by Wayland
Copyright © Hodder and Stoughton, 2020
All rights reserved
Series editor: Elise Short
Design: Wildpixel Ltd.

HB ISBN: 978 1 5263 0966 2
PB ISBN: 978 1 5263 0967 9

Printed and bound in China
Wayland, an imprint of
Hachette Children's Group
Part of Hodder and Stoughton
Carmelite House
50 Victoria Embankment
London EC4Y 0DZ
An Hachette UK Company
www.hachette.co.uk
www.hachettechildrens.co.uk

MIX
Paper from
responsible sources
FSC® C104740

Picture credits:
front cover gyn9037/Shutterstock, back cover DJI Creative Studio LLC (top
left), Open Government Licence (bottom right), Parrot (bottom right), 1 DJI
Creative Studio LLC (main), Evgeny Karandaev/Shutterstock (background),
2 Shaineast/Shutterstock (background), DJI Creative Studio LLC (main),
4-5 Supphaichai Salaeman/Shutterstock (background), 5 Sibsky2016/
Shutterstock (top), Defense Advanced Research Projects Agency (centre),
6-7 Apic/Getty Images, 6 National Museum of the U.S. Air Force (bottom),
7 U.S. Army/David Conover (top), Parrot (bottom), 12 Amazon (bottom
left), 12-13 Domino's Pizza Enterprises, 13 © 2018 United Parcel Service
of America, Inc. (top), Jeff Schear/Getty Images for Marriott (bottom), 14
Andy Burn/University of Reading, 14-15 Jag_cz/Shutterstock, 15 STR/AFP/
Getty Images (centre), Dmitry Kalinovsky (bottom), 16 U.S. Air Force (left),
BAE (right), 16-17 Defense Advanced Research Projects Agency, 17 Open
Government Licence (bottom), 18 Dmitry Dven/Shutterstock, 19 Bo Bridges/
Bad Robot/Skydance Prods/Paramount/Kobal/REX/Shutterstock (top), Jost
Jelovcan (bottom), 20 DJI Creative Studio LLC (top), AMF Photography/
Shutterstock (bottom), 20-21 Boris Mokousov/Shutterstock (background), 21
Peter Parks/Getty Images (top), Pierre Andrieu/AFP/Getty Images (bottom),
22-23 Mathias Kniepeiss/Getty Images, 23 Private Collection (top), Hep
Svadja/Make Magazine (centre), 24 Aerix (bottom), Jung Yeon-Je/AFP/
Getty Images, 25 Boeing (top), Racerx (centre), 26 Sakaret/Shutterstock, 27
Toshifumi Kitamura/AFP/Getty Images (top), Liteye UK (top centre), Georges
Gobet/AFP/Getty Images (bottom centre), Lukas Gojda/Shutterstock
(bottom), 28 Feng Zhoufeng/Southern Metropolis Daily/VCG via Getty
Images (top), Asiastock/Shutterstock (bottom), 29 Omer Messinger/EPA-
EFE/REX/Shutterstock (top), Stefan Niedermayr (centre)

Every attempt has been made to clear copyright. Should there
be any inadvertent omission please apply to the publisher for
rectification.

CONTENTS

WHAT IS A DRONE?

Drones are taking off, and in their millions! These remote-controlled unmanned aerial vehicles (UAVs) or multicopters, are now hugely popular for stunt-flying, racing, photography, professional film shoots and dazzling light shows.

INTO SERVICE

In this book you'll find out about the history of drone use, how a drone works, plus how to control one and obey aviation rules. You'll meet top drone racers and discover how UAVs are changing the way people work.

FROM TOY TO TOP-END

There are many types of UAVs on the market, from tiny toy models to heavyweight 'prosumer' kits that cost thousands. While most come ready assembled as Ready to Fly (RTF) models, you can also learn to build your own drone from a kit.

TIMELINE

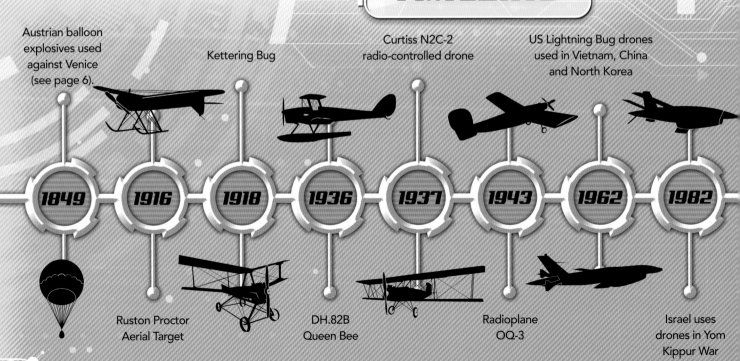

Austrian balloon explosives used against Venice (see page 6).

Kettering Bug

Curtiss N2C-2 radio-controlled drone

US Lightning Bug drones used in Vietnam, China and North Korea

1849 **1916** **1918** **1936** **1937** **1943** **1962** **1982**

Ruston Proctor Aerial Target

DH.82B Queen Bee

Radioplane OQ-3

Israel uses drones in Yom Kippur War

SPY IN THE SKY

UAVs have long had a part to play in the armed forces, spying from the air or carrying missiles. Discover what the latest defence drones can do and how tech firms are working to combat rogue drones, too.

LOOKING UP

And what of the future? Good or bad, drones are here to stay as drone sales rocket into the billions of dollars. With this book, you'll be prepared for the coming swarm.

RQ2 Pioneer, joint US/Israeli reconnaissance drone

First US commercial drone permit issued

Amazon announce plans to deliver by drone

MultiGP and Drone Racing League founded

1986 **1996** **2006** **2010** **2013** **2014** **2015** **2018**

MQ-1 Predator first deployed

Parrot AR Drone revealed at CES Las Vegas

DJI Phantom 1, camera-equipped UAV

Drones used for making films and TV programmes

Intel® Shooting Star™ system used in Winter Olympics

HISTORY OF THE DRONE

The first UAVs were designed for the armed forces, for use in target practice or spy missions. Now, with new affordable technology, flying drones has become a leisure and creative activity. Anyone can become a drone pilot.

THE FIRST DRONES?

The first record of UAVs used in war took place in 1849 when Austrian forces released hundreds of balloons to deliver timed explosives in a bold attack on Venice in modern-day Italy. Only one bomb hit the city, though, as the wind changed direction and blew the balloons off target.

AERIAL BUG

The **'Kettering Bug'** was a small unmanned biplane developed in the USA as an aerial torpedo in the First World War (1914–18). It used gyroscopic stabilisers to keep it level, while flying distance was calculated by counting the spins of its propeller. However, the 'Bug' was full of flaws; it often crashed and the war ended before it was used in combat.

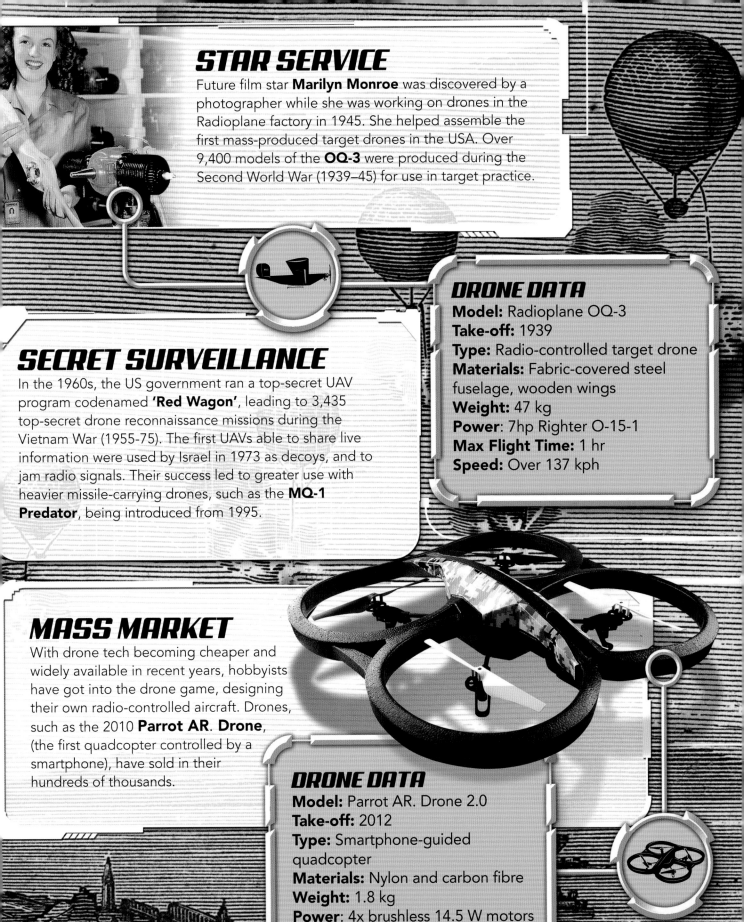

STAR SERVICE

Future film star **Marilyn Monroe** was discovered by a photographer while she was working on drones in the Radioplane factory in 1945. She helped assemble the first mass-produced target drones in the USA. Over 9,400 models of the **OQ-3** were produced during the Second World War (1939–45) for use in target practice.

DRONE DATA

Model: Radioplane OQ-3
Take-off: 1939
Type: Radio-controlled target drone
Materials: Fabric-covered steel fuselage, wooden wings
Weight: 47 kg
Power: 7hp Righter O-15-1
Max Flight Time: 1 hr
Speed: Over 137 kph

SECRET SURVEILLANCE

In the 1960s, the US government ran a top-secret UAV program codenamed **'Red Wagon'**, leading to 3,435 top-secret drone reconnaissance missions during the Vietnam War (1955-75). The first UAVs able to share live information were used by Israel in 1973 as decoys, and to jam radio signals. Their success led to greater use with heavier missile-carrying drones, such as the **MQ-1 Predator**, being introduced from 1995.

MASS MARKET

With drone tech becoming cheaper and widely available in recent years, hobbyists have got into the drone game, designing their own radio-controlled aircraft. Drones, such as the 2010 **Parrot AR. Drone**, (the first quadcopter controlled by a smartphone), have sold in their hundreds of thousands.

DRONE DATA

Model: Parrot AR. Drone 2.0
Take-off: 2012
Type: Smartphone-guided quadcopter
Materials: Nylon and carbon fibre
Weight: 1.8 kg
Power: 4x brushless 14.5 W motors
Max Flight Time: 15 mins
Speed: 40 kph

ANATOMY OF A DRONE

What makes up a drone? Here's a close-up look at the clever tech that keeps a quadcopter up in the air.

FRAME

The frame supports the mechanical parts of the drone. It needs to be light but sturdy, capable of surviving the occasional rough landing. Plastic and carbon fibres are often used. The **boom arms** that hold the propellers need to be thin to avoid getting in the way of the propellers' **downdraft**.

FLIGHT CONTROLLER

The drone's 'computer brain' keeps the drone stable and receives commands via radio or WiFi to change speed and direction. The flight controller sends signals to the **ESC (Electronic Speed Controller)** that changes the speed of each motor and propeller, and to the optional camera. The flight controller's sensors include a **gyroscope** for maintaining balance, an **accelerometer** for changing speed, a **barometer** for measuring altitude, and a **magnetometer** to recognise compass bearings.

CAMERA AND GIMBAL

Many drones carry a camera for aerial photography. The gimbal is a rotating mount that keeps the camera steady below the drone's frame.

PROPELLERS

The propellers are attached to the drone's motors. As they spin, they create the thrust to give a drone lift-off. The propeller blades have an **aerofoil** shape like aeroplane wings that helps produce lift.

MOTORS

Efficient, long-lasting motors, like those used in CD drives and computer fans, are the standard in drones. These are quick to react to commands for a change of speed or direction.

BATTERY

The battery is often the heaviest component. Light, rechargeable, batteries may only provide power for about 20 minutes. Longer-lasting batteries are heavier. Heavy UAVs consume more power so it's a trade-off between power and weight.

LANDING GEAR

The landing gear allows the drone to come back to earth gently without the propellers touching the ground.

UNDER CONTROL

Whatever UAV you choose, you will need to master the basic controls to keep your vehicle in the air and steady.

PRE-FLIGHT CHECK

- Check aviation rules about flying drones in your area.
- Check the weather. Don't fly in wet, foggy or very windy weather.
- Avoid busy areas or places with wires, trees and other obstructions.
- Check the battery is fully charged. (Spares are useful, too.)
- Check the frame and parts are secured.
- Take off to eye-level and hold for 15 seconds to check the drone is working.

TAKE-OFF AND LANDING

Push the **throttle** up gently to start the propellers and slowly lift the drone in a controlled way. Slowly bring the drone down to land and repeat to test systems are working correctly and that you can safely bring your drone back to earth.

MOVEMENT

- Keep your drone hovering at eye-level for a while, then test the **yaw** control, slowly turning the drone to face different directions (see opposite).
- Practise moving it backwards and forwards with the **pitch** control, then left and right with the **yaw** control.
- Once you're confident, pilot your drone in a square pattern using **pitch** and **roll**.
- The next step is to practise circular flight patterns, using the **pitch**, **roll** and **throttle**.

FIRST-PERSON VIEW

First-Person View (FPV) allows you to follow the movement of your drone via video goggles or a monitor connected to the drone's camera – a real bird's eye view.

IN SIGHT

You should always be able to see your drone in flight even, when you are using **FPV** to follow your drone's route.

AUTOPILOT

With the right apps and a Global Positioning System (GPS) module on top of your drone, you can pre-program a flight plan for your UAV. First, plot **waypoints** on a map, then set your drone to fly between them. You can also include an automatic return home in your flight plan.

CONTROLS

The four main quadcopter controls are:

Yaw – This rotates your quadcopter clockwise or anticlockwise

Roll – This moves your quadcopter left or right

Throttle – This starts the propellers to give your quadcopter lift

Pitch – This moves your quadcopter back and forth

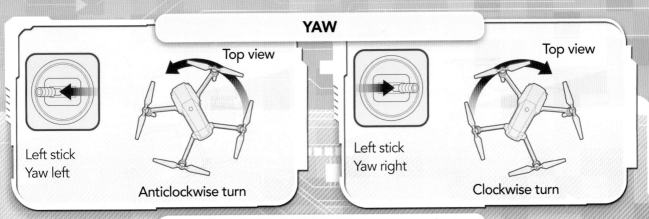

YAW

Left stick
Yaw left

Top view

Anticlockwise turn

Left stick
Yaw right

Top view

Clockwise turn

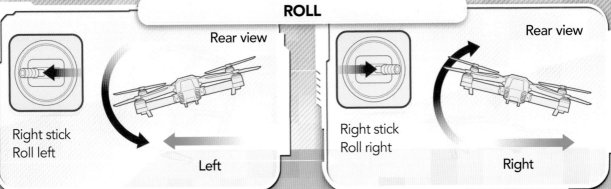

ROLL

Right stick
Roll left

Rear view

Left

Right stick
Roll right

Rear view

Right

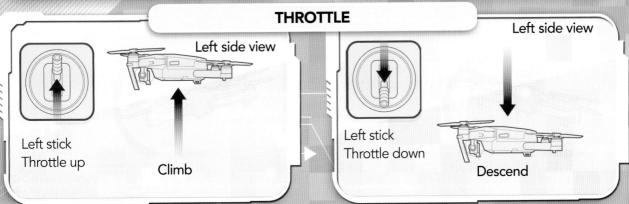

THROTTLE

Left stick
Throttle up

Left side view

Climb

Left stick
Throttle down

Left side view

Descend

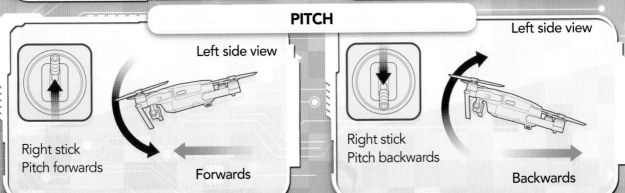

PITCH

Right stick
Pitch forwards

Left side view

Forwards

Right stick
Pitch backwards

Left side view

Backwards

DELIVERY DRONES

Got a craving for a pizza? Well, you could soon have it delivered to your door by drone. Major companies are starting to use drones not just to drop off takeaways but also urgent supplies, such as medicines.

THE DROP-OFF

Amazon was one of the first companies to see the potential of drones for getting products from A to B. **Amazon Prime Air** aims to deliver packages up to 2 kg in weight from warehouses to customers in 30 minutes or less using totally autonomous drones guided by GPS. The company has already successfully trialled the service in the UK, but doesn't have permission to use drone delivery yet.

DRONE DATA
Model: Flirtey DRU
Take-off: 2016
Type: Hexacopter
Materials: Carbon fibre, aluminium, 3D-printing
Cargo Weight: 2.5 kg
Speed: 30 kph

PIZZA TO GO

Domino's Pizza, New Zealand, has been testing UAVs for door-to-door deliveries using **Flirtey's DRU Drones**. The pizzas are lowered from a hovering drone to waiting customers using a detachable cable. Domino's have plans to offer the service in other countries soon.

OFF THE ROOF

Shipping service **UPS** has been testing drones by using the roofs of their vans as 'helipads'. They think that by using drones to reduce driving routes for each of the company's 66,000 delivery drivers they could save US$50 million.

HEALTHY OPTION

Based in Rwanda, the company **Zipline** uses drones to deliver urgent medicines, blood and vaccines directly to clinics in remote parts of the country where journeys over mountains and washed-out roads can be treacherous.

COCKTAIL HOUR

The Marriott Marquis Hotel in Chicago, USA has been pioneering waiter service for guests by delivering cocktails to tables. Other guests will have to watch their heads!

MAPPING THE WORLD

Having a bird's-eye view comes in handy for more than admiring scenery. Drones are useful tools for archaeologists, builders, farmers and even shop owners.

OUTLINE OF THE BUILDING

BURIED TREASURE

Drones can look back in time! By fitting a drone with a thermal camera, archaeologists have located hidden ancient sites, as buried structures appear a different temperature compared to the ground around them. One new drone discovery was this 5,600-year-old 'House of the Dead' under a field near Stonehenge in the UK.

A NEW CROP

Farmers can use drones to map and monitor their fields, even using sensors to find out if a crop needs water. Drones have the potential to take over many farmers' tasks, including spraying and planting. Start-up company **BioCarbon Engineering** has developed a system of drones that can plant 100,000 trees in a single day by releasing biodegradable seed pods into the soil.

RETAIL ROBOTS

Need help with your shopping? Hypermarket chain **Walmart** wants to use drones as in-store assistants. The retail giant has patented plans to have drones map the contents of a store and help shoppers locate the goods they need. First, they upload a shopping list from a smartphone or tablet, then they lead each shopper to the correct shelf.

CROWD CONTROL

Most major cities have CCTV cameras monitoring traffic and recording disturbances. The next step for police and traffic controllers is to use drones at big events, such as sports finals and marches. Drones can arrive at a scene early and relay footage of any potential trouble. Drones are also used by law enforcers to patrol properties and borders between countries.

HIGH RISE

Drones are changing the way the construction industry works, too. Before building begins, drones can survey land. During construction, they can record and monitor progress and check safety standards. Once a building is complete, a drone fly-past film or video will impress possible buyers. For existing buildings, a survey by a drone is a speedy way of assessing any damage and the need for any repair work.

MILITARY DRONES

Drones have become hugely important on the field of battle, for armed forces surveillance, and the delivery of deadly cargos.

DRONE OF PREY

The **Predator** has been in service in various forms for the United States Air Force for 23 years, following its 1995 launch. Originally a **reconnaissance** craft with cameras and sensors, from 2004 the **MQ-1A** and its successor the **MQ-9 'Reaper'** were upgraded to carry two Hellfire missiles to the enemy. The drone and its weapon launches are remotely controlled.

DRONE DATA

Model: BAE Systems Taranis Drone
Take-off: 2013
Type: Unmanned warplane
Power: Rolls-Royce Adour Moderate by-pass ratio turbofan engine
Wingspan: 10 m
Weight: 512 kg unloaded
Max Speed: Mach 1

GROUND CONTROL

The Predator is guided from a remote base via satellite link. Two crew members control it: a pilot to guide the drone and command the mission, and another aircrew member to operate the drone's sensors and weapons.

STEALTH MISSION

For stealth missions, the UK plans to employ the **BAE Systems Taranis Drone**. Tested in 2013, this potentially supersonic UAV carries shielded weapon bays to avoid radar detection. It can be controlled via satellite link from anywhere on Earth and is programmed to deliver weapons and automatically defend itself from both manned and unmanned enemy attacks.

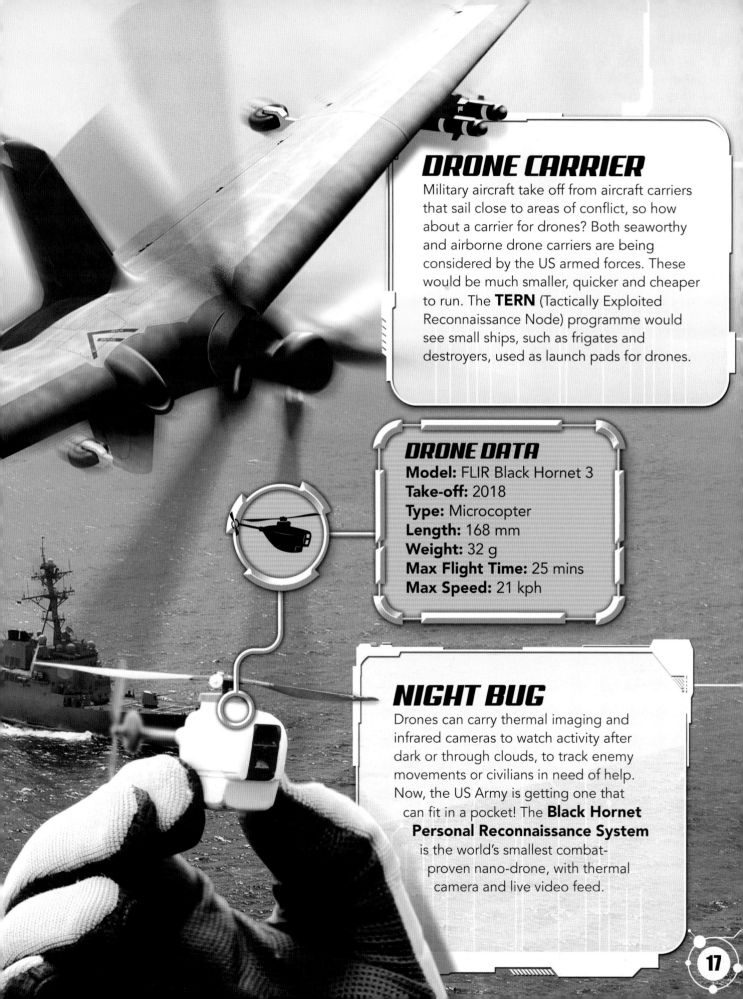

DRONE CARRIER

Military aircraft take off from aircraft carriers that sail close to areas of conflict, so how about a carrier for drones? Both seaworthy and airborne drone carriers are being considered by the US armed forces. These would be much smaller, quicker and cheaper to run. The **TERN** (Tactically Exploited Reconnaissance Node) programme would see small ships, such as frigates and destroyers, used as launch pads for drones.

DRONE DATA

Model: FLIR Black Hornet 3
Take-off: 2018
Type: Microcopter
Length: 168 mm
Weight: 32 g
Max Flight Time: 25 mins
Max Speed: 21 kph

NIGHT BUG

Drones can carry thermal imaging and infrared cameras to watch activity after dark or through clouds, to track enemy movements or civilians in need of help. Now, the US Army is getting one that can fit in a pocket! The **Black Hornet Personal Reconnaissance System** is the world's smallest combat-proven nano-drone, with thermal camera and live video feed.

EYE IN THE SKY

A big draw for owning a drone is aerial photography. With the right camera kit and practice, you could end up joining the professionals, filming wildlife documentaries or Hollywood action scenes.

GET THE KIT

As a budding director you will need a motorised **gimbal** to hold the camera beneath your multicopter and to direct it during a flight.

Do research to work out the best camera for your needs: do you need HD-quality, fast-frame rates or something cheap and cheerful for home videos? **GoPro** cornered the early market in lightweight cameras for capturing dramatic action, on helmets, bike handlebars, and now drones, but there are many options out there, with some drone manufacturers making their own cameras.

CALLING THE SHOTS

Once you've got the kit, here are three video shots you should practise.

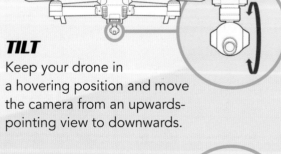

TILT

Keep your drone in a hovering position and move the camera from an upwards-pointing view to downwards.

TRACKING SHOT

Choose a static subject, such as a building. Keep the camera still, at 45 degrees to the subject as your drone passes by smoothly.

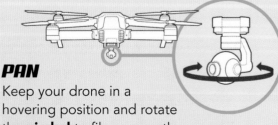

PAN

Keep your drone in a hovering position and rotate the **gimbal** to film a smooth horizontal shot.

BLOCKBUSTER BUSINESS

Hollywood has taken up drones in a big way, using them to capture dramatic aerial shots and to follow rapid chases in films, such as the **Marvel**, **Mission: Impossible**, **James Bond** and the **Harry Potter** series. Using drones with professional pilots allows directors to record these fast-paced scenes from a lower level and closer than would be possible from a helicopter.

AHEAD OF THE HERD

The classic introduction to a nature documentary has the camera sweeping over a landscape, or tracking a herd of wild animals. Many of these scenes used to be shot from light aircraft. Now, professional drone camera operators call the shots. Drones are cheaper to use, less intrusive and can reach remote spots without the need for a landing strip. It's also much safer than sending a camera operator near a pride of lions!

TO THE RESCUE

Drones save lives. Emergency services use UAVs to help monitor dangerous situations, help locate people and animals and deliver rescue equipment.

SEARCH AND FIND

Drones are ideal for aerial search operations. Launched in minutes, they can provide live images and cover ground that emergency services would struggle to reach. GPS information can be relayed back to base instantly to direct crews to find missing people. In 2018, when 65-year-old climber Rick Allen fell during a solo attempt on the 8,000 m Broad Peak in Pakistan's Karokorum Range, he was presumed dead. But, a high-altitude **DJI Mavic Pro** drone spotted him on the slopes and guided a rescue that brought him down safety for a full recovery.

STORM DAMAGE

Following the devastating Hurricane Harvey that hit the USA in 2017, a fleet of drones was sent to assess the damage in Houston, Texas, where more than 30,000 houses were flooded. They were quickly able to check homes, offices, roads, bridges and power lines and help emergency services decide when it was safe to return. Insurance companies followed with their own drones to check out compensation claims.

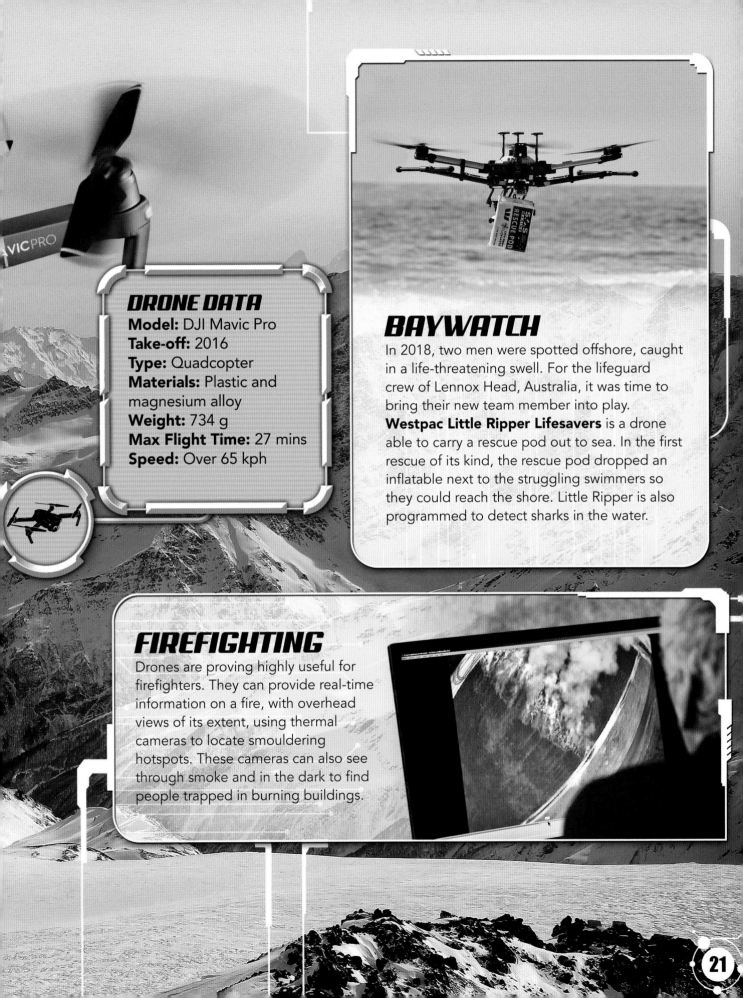

DRONE DATA

Model: DJI Mavic Pro
Take-off: 2016
Type: Quadcopter
Materials: Plastic and magnesium alloy
Weight: 734 g
Max Flight Time: 27 mins
Speed: Over 65 kph

BAYWATCH

In 2018, two men were spotted offshore, caught in a life-threatening swell. For the lifeguard crew of Lennox Head, Australia, it was time to bring their new team member into play. **Westpac Little Ripper Lifesavers** is a drone able to carry a rescue pod out to sea. In the first rescue of its kind, the rescue pod dropped an inflatable next to the struggling swimmers so they could reach the shore. Little Ripper is also programmed to detect sharks in the water.

FIREFIGHTING

Drones are proving highly useful for firefighters. They can provide real-time information on a fire, with overhead views of its extent, using thermal cameras to locate smouldering hotspots. These cameras can also see through smoke and in the dark to find people trapped in burning buildings.

THE RACE IS ON

Drone racing is one of the fastest-growing sports in the world – a dazzling, high-octane spectacle for millions of fans, with prizes worth hundreds of thousands of dollars for the most daring and skilful pilots.

MULTIGP

Drone owners love to pit their skills against one another and **MultiGP** lets them do just that in an organised international league. MultiGP sets up radio-controlled drone races and invites pilots of any level to join local division of MultiGP and improve their piloting skills in classes.

THE LEAGUE

The **Drone Racing League** (DRL) was founded in the USA in 2015. DRL races involve pilots using **First-Person View** (see page 10) to guide identical drones through 3D courses at speeds up to 128 kph. The first races broadcast on TV had pilots charge through obstacle courses in shopping centres, stadiums, laboratories and car factories.

ACCELERATE

Car manufacturer BMW is working with the DRL to break the record for the world's fastest racing drone. Drones are being tested in the BMW wind tunnel at its Aerodynamic Test Centre to help break the league's own record.

AIR ACE

Carlos 'Charpu' Puertolas was one of the first superstar racers to hit the drone racing scene. An animator by day, Charpu's acrobatic UAV videos are a hit online, though now he races mostly for fun.

FREESTYLING

When **Zoe Stumbaugh** became ill and had to spend two years in bed, she took up a new hobby – flying micro drones. Now she's a top drone designer and winning racer, working on the world's smallest racing drone and perfecting new freestyle flying moves.

WORLD CUP

Drone racing has its own world cup too, launched by the Fédération Aéronautique Internationale (FAI) in 2016. Pilots compete with quadcopters under 1 kg in weight through specially built courses. The 2018 World Cup competition crossed continents with more than 20 international events, starting on the island of Bali, Indonesia.

ALL-STARS

Swarms of sparkling drones, thumb-sized quadcopters or super-fast racers ... Drone designers and pilots are pushing the boundaries of what is possible, breaking records and stunning spectators with aerial light shows.

COOL CONSTELLATION

The **Olympic Games** is one of the most-watched sports events in the world, and the pressure to put on a spectacular opening show is huge. For the 2018 Winter Olympics in PyeongChang, South Korea, they had just the answer: send in the drones!

The **Intel® Shooting Star™** drone system amazed viewers with a spectacular display of 1,218 light-emitting quadcopters above the opening ceremony.

A central computer coordinated the swarm of drones with four billion LED light combinations animating a giant mid-air snowboarder, which transformed into the famous Olympic rings.

kph

INSECT SIZED

How small can a drone go? At 3 x 3 x 2 cm, the **Aerius Quadcopter** is so tiny, it can balance on your fingertip! This minute, toy-like drone can manage up to seven minutes flying on a 15-minute charge. It's an engineering marvel and a ton of fun, with pre-programmed aerobatic tricks and LED lights.

DRONE DATA

Model: Intel® Shooting Star™
Take-off: 2016
Type: Quadcopter
Materials: Plastic, foam
Weight: 330 g
Max Flight Time: 20 mins
Max Range: 1.5 km
Speed: 10.8 kph

HEAVY LOAD

Pizzas and doughnuts are light loads, but what if you want to use a drone to deliver something much heavier? **Boeing's** aerospace engineers have the solution – a massive unmanned prototype with eight propellers, each 1.8 m in length. The tech wizards are aiming to get this car-sized beast delivering 225 kg of cargo – the weight of a grizzly bear – at speeds of up to 112 kph.

DRONE DATA

Model: DRL RacerX
Take-off: 2017
Type: Quadcopter
Materials: 3D-printed thermoplastic polyurethane (TPU), carbon fibre, copper wire and fasteners
Weight: 800 g
Motors: 4 x T-motor F80
Speed: 289 kph

BREAKING SPEED LIMITS

The **Drone Racing League** has strict rules on how fast a drone can fly in a competition, but that hasn't stopped its designers breaking records. Tested on a 100 m course, the **DRL RacerX** topped 263 kph but has managed a whopping 289 kph over longer distances. Earlier test models burst into flames at high speeds!

Cheetah		121 kph
Average helicopter		257 kph
DRL RacerX		289 kph
Formula One car		300 kph

THE WAR ON DRONES

As with all new tech, there are concerns about drone safety and misuse. With the skies getting crowded, rules have to be followed to avoid collisions and invasions of privacy. Some people have taken unusual steps to stop drones getting close.

THE LAW ON DRONES

Rules about drone usage have been introduced in many countries to avoid accidents and to protect people's privacy from hovering cameras. Regulations differ from country to country – and in some countries drones are illegal. Here are the basic rules for recreational drone users.

- You are responsible for flying your drone in a safe manner.

- You must keep the drone in your direct sight at all times while it is flying.

- Flying of private drones is forbidden in congested areas, near military bases and airfields – where drones could collide with planes during take-off and landing.

- Pilots of drones weighing over certain weights need to get a licence by passing a course. (Over 25 kg in the USA, 20 kg in the UK.)

- There may be limits on the height you can fly your drone. (120 m in the USA and UK.)

- Respect people's privacy when using a drone with a camera. Let people know you are filming and think before sharing online.

Check the rules for your country before using your drone.

NO DRONE ZONE

NORSIGN (N.T.) · Ph: (X8 8847 07

TANGLED UP

In Tokyo, Japan, no-fly zones, such as the Imperial Palace and prime minister's office, are patrolled by large **interceptor drones** carrying cameras and nets 2–3 m in length that can scoop–up rogue UAVs in mid-air.

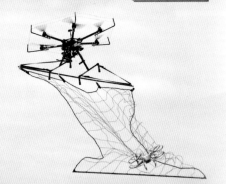

DEATH RAYS

Tech firm **Liteye Systems** have designed an **Anti-UAV Defense System** (AUDS) which blocks radio signals used to control any passing drone. Boeing have built the even-more-direct **Compact Laser Weapons System** that fires a two-kilowatt laser, which can burn a hole in a UAV.

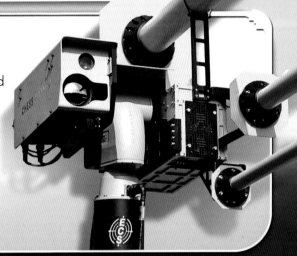

FEATHERED FURY

Following a two-year trial with eagles by Dutch police, both US and Russian security teams are training falcons to attack drones that enter prohibited airspace.

AIR ALERT

New York's Newark, and London's Heathrow and Gatwick airports were all closed temporarily in 2018 and 2019 due to drone sightings. At Gatwick, 1,000 flights had to be cancelled or diverted over three days due to fears that drones may interfere with aircraft taking off and landing. The airports are investing millions in anti-drone equipment.

INTO THE FUTURE

Are drones snooping, robotic killing machines or a great bit of kit for practising piloting skills and making cool films? A bit of both really. Here's what you can expect to see from UAVs in the near future.

DRONE DATA

Model: EHang 184
Type: Quadcopter
Materials: Reinforced composite material, carbon fibre, epoxy
Length: 4 m
Weight: 260 kg
Passengers: One
Max Flight Time: 25 mins
Speed: 100 kph

DRONE SCHOOL

Knowing how to safely pilot a drone may become as essential as learning to drive a car. In Seoul, South Korea, there are already public drone parks available for new UAV owners to take classes and practise skills.

PILOT-FREE PASSAGE

Just as driverless cars are being tested on public roads, pilotless planes are being tested for the skies. Single and two-passenger drones, such as the electrically powered **EHang 184**, **Volocopter 2X** and **Airbus Vahana VTOL**, have proved it possible. Larger commercial flights could also be operated remotely without a pilot in the cockpit.

24-HOUR WATCH

Drone cameras can be fitted with facial-recognition software to trace and track the movements of criminals. With links to police databases, they can be used to hunt for suspects in crowds. You may not even realise you're being followed!

PORTABLE PAL

You need never be without a drone. Micro drones, like the in-development **Nixie**, can be worn on the wrist like a bracelet. This tiny wearable device will unfold into a quadcopter, including a camera. The Nixie could be controlled from a smartphone and pre-programmed to return to its owner after a flight.

IMITATION GAME

Drones that look like birds of prey are already being used to scare away other birds from airport flight paths. Spy agencies could also employ drones that imitate birds and insects, to watch suspects. What may seem like a bee or hummingbird buzzing about you could really be a flying camera, recording your every move!

distributed computer system GPS, GSM, Wi-Fi, sensors

wing flapping and tilting

batteries

head/beak camera

Whatever the future holds for UAV technology, it's sure to impact on our lives in a big way, as a toy, a pest, a weapon or a tool. The sky's the limit, and it's filling with drones!

GLOSSARY

Accelerometer A device for measuring speed

Altitude Height above sea level

Autonomous Able to control itself without external commands

Barometer A device that works out altitude by measuring air pressure

Boom The part of the frame that holds a UAV's propeller

Downdraft Downward current of air, as created by a spinning horizontal propeller

Drone Common name for UAV

ESC Electronic Speed Controller that links a drone's flight controller and motor to control speed

FPV (First-Person View) Use of a monitor or video goggles connected to a drone's camera to pilot a drone

Fuselage Main body of an aircraft

Gimbal A motorised camera mount

GPS (Global Positioning System) Navigation system based on signals from orbiting satellites

Gyroscope A device for measuring orientation

Hexacopter A multicopter with six propellers

Jam To stop radio signals from reaching the people who want to receive them

Magnetometer Instrument that measures magnetic forces to work out compass bearings

Multicopter A UAV with several propellers

Pitch Front and back tilt that moves your drone forwards and backwards

Prosumer Buyer choosing higher-end professional models

Quadcopter A multicopter with four propellers

Reconnaissance Military observation of an area

Roll Rotation that moves your drone left or right

RTF (Ready to Fly) A ready-built drone that you can fly straight from the box

Surveillance Close observation, spying

Throttle Control that increases or decreases propeller spin making a drone go up or down

UAV Unmanned Aerial Vehicle

Waypoint Point marked on a path

Yaw Clockwise or anticlockwise rotation

USEFUL SITES

Civil Aviation Authority, UK
Info about all aspects of unmanned aviation: caa.co.uk/consumers/unmanned-aircraft-and-drones/

Dronethusiast
Drone news for and by enthusiasts: dronethusiast.com

Drone Girl
UAV news and reviews from Sally French: thedronegirl.com

Drone Racing League
Professional drone-racing: thedroneracingleague.com

Federal Aviation Administration
US drone-flying tips and regulations: faa.gov/uas/getting_started/

MultiGP
Largest professional drone racing league in the world: multigp.com

My First Drone
Buying tips for new UAV pilots: myfirstdrone.com

That Drone Show
Drone video reviews from the founders of International Drone Day: thatdroneshow.com

UAV Coach
Drone pilot training classes: uavcoach.com/

Wired
New developments about UAVs from top tech mag: wired.co.uk/topic/drones

USEFUL BOOKS

The Complete Guide to Drones, Adam Juniper (Octopus, 2015)

The Drones Book (Future)

Build Your Own Drone Manual, Alex Elliott (Haynes, 2016)

INDEX